Contribitors

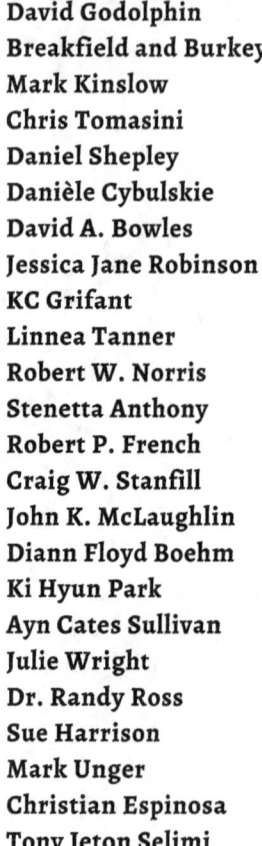

David Godolphin
Breakfield and Burkey
Mark Kinslow
Chris Tomasini
Daniel Shepley
Danièle Cybulskie
David A. Bowles
Jessica Jane Robinson
KC Grifant
Linnea Tanner
Robert W. Norris
Stenetta Anthony
Robert P. French
Craig W. Stanfill
John K. McLaughlin
Diann Floyd Boehm
Ki Hyun Park
Ayn Cates Sullivan
Julie Wright
Dr. Randy Ross
Sue Harrison
Mark Unger
Christian Espinosa
Tony Jeton Selimi

Special thanks to:
Scott Hughes
Onlinebookclub.org

Founder & Editor in Chief: S. Jeyran Main
Publisher: Review Tales Publishing &
Editing Services
Print & Distribution: IngramSparks
Cover Photo: Moldy Vintages
Designs: Pexels
ISBN 978-1-988680-30-9 (Paperback)
ISBN 978-1-988680-31-6 (Digital)
www.jeyranmain.com
For all inquiries, please get in touch with us
directly.

A BOOK MAGAZINE FOR INDIE AUTHORS

REVIEW TALES

TABLE OF CONTENTS

Editor's
Notes

We welcome Spring 2023 with open arms. The 6th edition of this magazine is filled with many delightful and insightful submissions. Mark Kinslow shares how his book was accidentally created without him ever thinking of becoming an author. Chris Tomasini confesses how liberating the writing experience has been.

We have interviewed some esteemed authors with tremendous potential and, with that, understand what it takes to be a writer. Character development, writer's block, writing quirks, and everything that matters in this industry are discussed in detail.

Above all, I am incredibly proud and delighted to see the support and togetherness this magazine has caused. What exists here and what we have accomplished is a beautiful team effort of those passionate and caring to keep such a platform alive.

I thank you all, and keep writing!

Jeyran Main

Founder & Editor-in-chief
Review Tales Magazine - Publishing & Editing Services

Author Confessions

David Godolphin's Soap-Stud & Blue-Movie Girl has been described by one reader as 'a potent Tinseltown cocktail with a slice of Jackie Collins and a dash of Gore Vidal.' I am happy to admit to those influences, but I say that my all-time favorite Hollywood author is Harold Robbins, whose novels were deemed too racy for UK readers in the 1950s and 60s

"My Journey"

-David Godolphin

and she had to be expurgated for British editions. I acknowledge Thomas Tryon as another influence: Tryon's Crowned Heads and All That Glitters were collections of linked novellas about Hollywood actors and actresses with strong echoes of real stars. Soap-Stud & Blue-Movie Girl is two short novels yoked together. Soap-Stud charts the rise to TV fame of Jason Howl, a hunky lifeguard from San Diego whose career takes off after footage from a nude scene is posted online. Blue-Movie Girl is the rise to infamy of Joylene Duchat, a mixed-race beauty from Arizona. The daughter of a televangelist, Joylene seduces one of her teachers at 14 and becomes the new Queen of Porn at 18, although she really yearns to be a serious actress.

The idea of a girl with serious acting talent and aspirations settling for a career in porno was inspired by Joan Crawford, although Joan, bless her, always insisted that those rumors weren't true. I'm unsure why I made Joylene mixed-race — maybe to make her "exotic." I'd already written two drafts of the book when I first saw Meghan Markle on TV. I'm guessing the Duchess won't want to resume her acting career by playing Joylene Duchat — oh, happy thought! — I decided to turn Blue-Movie Girl into a streaming series like Sex Education, but she's precisely the intelligent and sassy actress I wanted Joylene to be.

'A London friend who introduced me to Diana was Cecil Brock, an Irish actor who'd started in repertory theatre with James Mason in the 1950s. Cecil appears in Blue-Movie Girl, playing Judge Jeffreys in a new comedy life of Nell Gwynne, which is Joylene's first role outside porn. Peter O'Toole plays Charles the Second; his queen is played by Dame Helen Highwater, who isn't intended to be any of the Dames you might think she is. And Cecil was dead when I cast him in Poor Nellie.' I have had a blast writing and continue to do so.

A three-generation family organization, the R-Group, was formed after Germany invaded Poland in 1939. The founding fathers' goal was to protect the innocent and correct injustices. The original modern-day, contemporary Enigma Series added a subgroup from the beloved characters called the Cyber Assassins Technology Services (CATS) team.

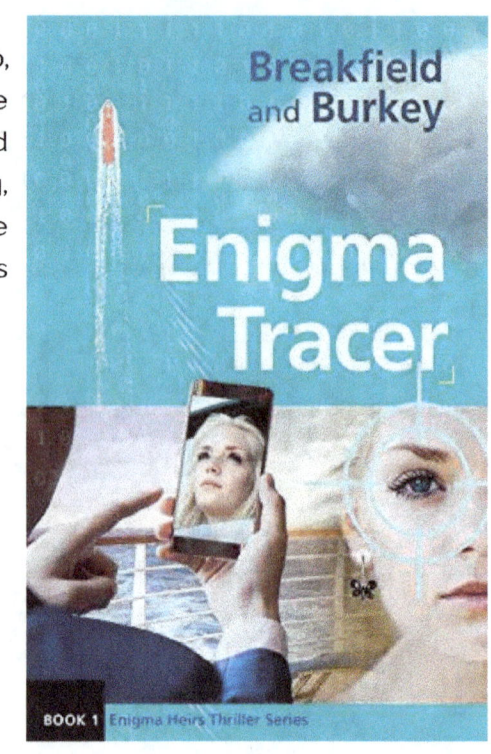

"Seeking the Best Value While Facing the Beasts"

-Breakfield and Burkey

We wanted to continue the series on both tracks while allowing the younger generation of family members to solve threats from the darknet associations. The Enigma Series contained twelve books, with two focused on the CATS.

We took that premise to form the new series Enigma Heirs to continue the modern-day fight of the cyber heroes versus the scum cyber thugs using the characteristics of both tracks. We put the twins, Gracie and Juan, in charge of each respective group to gain a new vantage point for the YA and beyond readers and listeners. We want readers to acquire ways to protect themselves while traversing the Internet and delivering compelling TechnoThrillers through our love of storytelling.

Our collection of novels expanded to include short stories and novellas as readers made requests. It allows us to flex our storytelling muscles and expand our readers to include mystery, women's contemporary, and even a few modern romance fans. The road is long and winding, with changes made along our journey as small press authors. Storytelling and publishing are part of the process, while marketing is the other. Learning and honing our marketing skills is more complex and challenging in many ways. We must stay abreast of new social media methods yet focus on what provides our fans with the best value. We like feedback from readers, and we take it to heart.

We need and want reviews for all our ebook, paperback, and audiobook formats. Our website is the doorway to our books and avenues to connect. Our website has an assortment of downloads for fun and samples of our stories.

Reach out anytime to Authors@EnigmaSeries.com.

I never wanted to be a writer or dreamed about publishing a book, and I am actually a slow reader. After a hilarious conversation with my mom, I just recently discovered that I was a terrible writer when I was a kid, so naturally, becoming an author has never been on my to-do list. Why did I write a book, then?

"How I Accidentally Wrote a Book"

-Mark Kinslow

Well, it all started a few years ago after I had hit a pretty low point in my life. I knew I needed to make some changes but struggled with where to start, so I turned to the self-help world for guidance. I began reading self-improvement books, listening to inspirational podcasts, and absorbing as much information as possible. As I worked on reinventing myself, I started to fall in love with the topic of self-help. I took notes, developed my own theories, and mapped out a path to find my version of happiness and success.

Several months later, I had an unbelievable and unexpected moment of clarity. In my pursuit of happiness, I realized that I had become extremely knowledgeable and passionate about the self-help field. I was able to change my life because of my persistent research and curiosity, and I wanted to share my knowledge and experience with others. I knew right then that not only did I want to write a book, but that I had already started. All of my research, notes, and theories that I had been formulating and testing along the way became the foundation of what would eventually become my first published book- Step By Step: The 7 Key Steps to Finding Happiness in the Pursuit of Success.

Except for becoming a father and that one time I successfully parallel parked my car on the first attempt, writing a book has been one of the most challenging and rewarding achievements of my life. I stumbled into this journey with no background, experience, or expectations, and I came out on the other side with an entirely new perspective on writing. I always assumed writing was reserved for professionals, English majors, and the wildly gifted, but I know that is untrue. I learned that the key to great writing is passion.

In December 2021, I pulled a coil-bound paper manuscript from my filing cabinet and self-published it as Close Your Eyes: A Fairy Tale. The book was written circa the year 2000 and had lain in the shadows for nearly 20 years before it saw the light of day. In the late 1990s and early 2000s, I tried very hard to find traditional publishers for my novella Festival and Close Your Eyes.

"My Confession"

-Chris Tomasini

Unable to do so, and at the time ignorant as to how self-publishing might have worked in 2000, I somewhat took a deep breath and decided to go to grad school, get a career, and a family, and all of those sorts of things that you are unable to do when you're living in dismal basement apartments in Toronto, working minimum wage jobs, and spending all your free time writing.

In 2015, having heard about Amazon's CreateSpace program, I self-published Festival, thinking it was the more substantial book. I left Close Your Eyes in the filing cabinet, perhaps because I was still unsure what exactly I had written with that hard-to-describe and genre-defying book. However, partly hoping that some "buzz" from Close Your Eyes might help me find a publisher for the Within This Darkness young adult trilogy I'd been writing, I brought Close Your Eyes into the light of day. And I'm glad I did. After a year, and numerous promotional efforts, such as GoodReads giveaways, having the book on NetGalley, contacting book bloggers, etc., Close Your Eyes currently has a 4.65 average on Goodreads and has been called "a classic in the making" by the Historical Fiction Company.

Out of this darkness and into the light? Perhaps. Or it was the right time for a gently and mysteriously told book about love and kindness to hit the shelves.

05

Author Interviews

THE OTHER SIDE OF SANITY

BY DANIEL SHEPLEY

WHEN DID YOU FIRST REALIZE YOU WANTED TO BE A WRITER?

In my life, I have been in two counseling situations. My first experience with psychologists ended very negatively for me, so I pursued my grievances through legal and illegal means. After my lawsuit ended, I began counseling with a psychiatrist.

My psychiatrist had me write down what I was thinking and feeling. He called this "diaristic therapy." After years of doing this, he encouraged me to convert my notes into a book to hopefully help others who – like I was then – are "on the edge" and are considering committing murder or suicide, or both.

HOW DO YOU SCHEDULE YOUR LIFE WHEN YOU'RE WRITING?

When I published The Other Side of Sanity, I lived in Texas. Shortly after going to print, I moved home to Pennsylvania to help my aging parents, who had health issues. Sadly, my father went to heaven in July, so I'm now focused on caring for mom.

Like most new writers, I have a day job where I typically telework from 6:30 AM to around 3:15 PM. When I can, I dedicate the next two hours to outlining, plotting, developing characters, and storytelling.

WHAT WOULD YOU SAY IS YOUR INTERESTING WRITING QUIRK?

An interesting writing quirk is that I'm strong on dialogue and action but slightly weak on robust character development. The "common man" feedback The Other Side of Sanity has received is that it is hard to put down. The "critical literary" feedback it has received is that I should have developed my characters more.

You'll like my book if you are an entertainment-oriented reader who enjoys a good action-based psychological mystery, thriller, or suspense story. On the other hand, if you are an in-depth character-focused, character-emotion reader, maybe not so much.

HOW TO LIVE LIKE A MONK: MEDIEVAL WISDOM FOR MODERN LIFE

BY DANIÈLE CYBULSKIE

WHAT DO YOU LIKE TO DO WHEN YOU'RE NOT WRITING?

When I'm not writing, I'm reading. I like to read fiction and non-fiction, although I avoid medieval stuff to give myself a break when I'm not working. I also enjoy walking my dog and doing krav maga and yoga (not simultaneously). I'm a lot like the monks in my book: I like spending quiet time alone, being in nature, and learning new things.

WHAT WAS ONE OF THE MOST SURPRISING THINGS YOU LEARNED IN CREATING YOUR BOOK?

Because medieval monks were meant to live a rigorous and austere lifestyle, I expected they'd advocate for pushing yourself to your limits in their writing. Instead, it's the opposite: monks were advised to take breaks and not to be too overzealous in their austerity. Monks understood, as we do, that overdoing it will lead to burnout, making it hard to accomplish anything. There are many places where monastic advice dovetails with modern research on wellness – that's the book's whole premise, after all – but this was one I didn't expect.

IS THERE ANYTHING YOU WOULD LIKE TO CONFESS ABOUT AS AN AUTHOR?

I didn't call myself an author for a long time because I never had the urge to sit down and write for writing's sake. But I always felt compelled to share what I'd learned out of sheer enthusiasm for medieval history, and the vehicle through which I could reach people was through writing. I still don't feel like a writer's writer – the person who can't wait to wake up and hit the keyboard. I feel much more like a teacher or a friend who has something interesting to tell you, and writing is the tool I use.

07

SHERIFF OF STARR COUNTY

BY DAVID A. BOWLES

WHEN DID YOU FIRST REALIZE YOU WANTED TO BE A WRITER?

As a young boy, I always had a vivid imagination. I watched people and began to write about them. I drew pictures of them long before I could write. This was before personal computers. I had a Big Chief tablet and a number 2 pencil. Few will understand, but it was required in my day—two lines instead of one on the tablet. Capital letters went to the top line, lowercase the bottom line. That's how I learned cursive writing. In the third grade, I wrote a story that my teacher showed all over the school. From then on, I was determined to be a writer.

WHERE DID YOU GET YOUR INFORMATION OR IDEA FOR YOUR BOOK?

Researching my family history led me to write their story in five novels. Sheriff of Starr County, the latest book in the Westward Sagas Series, the sequel to Comanche Trace, is the true story of my great-grandmother's nine-year-old cousin abducted by Comanche Indians on Shoal Creek Austin, Texas, in 1841. Her uncle Will, a Texas Ranger, sets out alone to find Fayette. Will and Fayette are not united until 1850 in Washington on the Brazos, Texas.

WHAT DO YOU LIKE TO DO WHEN YOU'RE NOT WRITING?

I travel with my companion dog Becka a six-year-old lab looking for something or someone to write about. I usually find a good story. If I write a scene in my book, I have been there. It's fun to travel the traces and trails my ancestors followed west. I can describe the color of the dirt and the valley in great detail. When I'm not writing, I'm thinking about writing.

AS A CHILD, WHAT DID YOU WANT TO DO WHEN YOU GREW UP?

Ranching was four generations before I did. I was the last generation in my family to raise cattle.

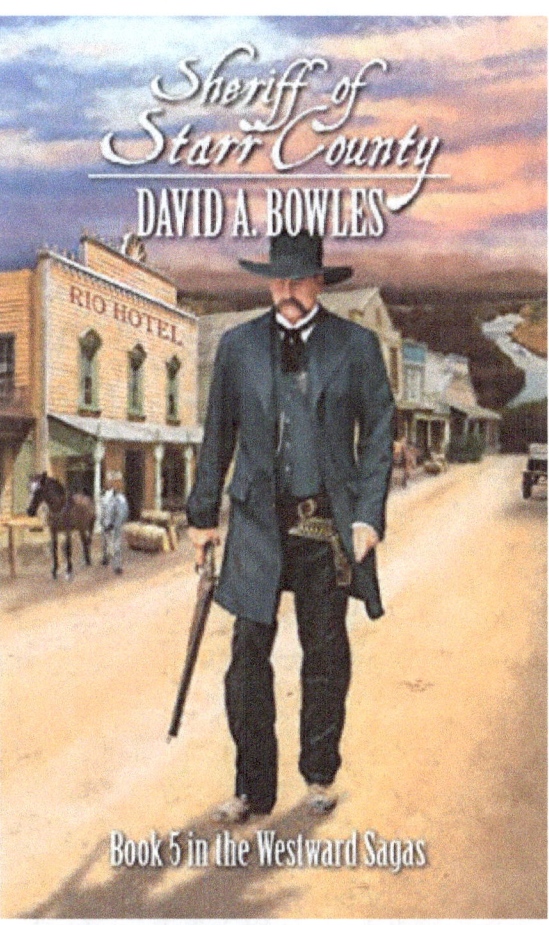

ORIGINS OF RESILIENCE

BY JESSICA JANE ROBINSON

HOW DO YOU SCHEDULE YOUR LIFE WHEN YOU'RE WRITING?

When I write Resilience Birthright Saga, I do my best to clear my schedule without interruptions. During 2014 when I was writing the first series of chapters, I would wake up at 4 am, meditate until 4:30 am, and write until 7:30 am/8 am. The four hours were a sweet spot because the house would be quiet. Working until 8 am was perfect because I could start regular work and have a productive day. My everyday responsibilities and dreams got the attention they needed for me to succeed.

HOW DID YOU GET YOUR BOOK PUBLISHED?

I went through the self-publishing route for "Origins of Resilience" and used the Lulu self-publishing platform. The most challenging part of publishing my graphic novel was finding the right artist to complete the illustrations within my budget. I got lucky with Charlo Nocete; he cut me a deal because he liked the environmental cause.

WHERE DID YOU GET YOUR INFORMATION OR IDEA FOR YOUR BOOK?

Before I started writing my graphic novel series, I had a superhero persona and a short film called "Recycle Woman" (available on YouTube). I showed "Recycle Woman" to my advisor Vince DeQuattro (who used to work for Industrial Light and Magic), in 2012. He told me the name Recycle Woman would get very little attention, though he liked the concept of my short film. He advised me to rename my superhero and write a comic because every superhero has one. At the same time I was following Vince's direction, I also became one of Former Vice President Al Gore's Climate Leaders. I began researching climate change and the destruction of the planet's natural habitats. It was during this time that I realized that my superhero needed to be more dynamic, and being boxed into just recycling wasn't going to allow my superhero the ability to address the complexities behind the environment's devastation.

09

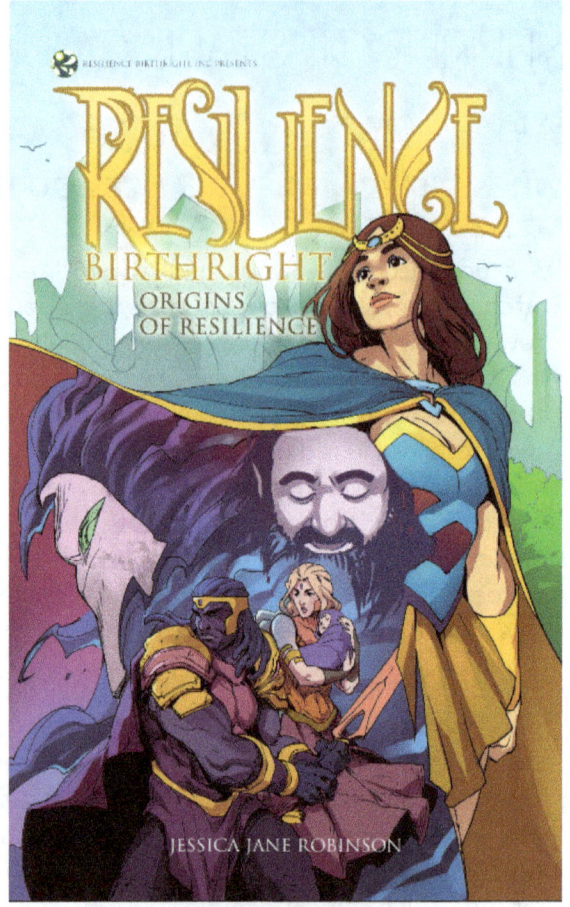

MELINDA WEST: MONSTER GUNSLINGER

BY KC GRIFANT

WHEN DID YOU FIRST REALIZE YOU WANTED TO BE A WRITER

I wanted to be a writer very early — pretty much as soon as I learned to put together sentences on the page successfully. I wrote sci-fi/fantasy tales as early as third or fourth grade. The very first story I recall writing was about a girl who shrunk down in size to soar on a paper plane. In middle and high school, I created adventure, fantasy, sci-fi, and horror stories (original and fan fiction), filling up dozens of composition notebooks.

HOW DO YOU SCHEDULE YOUR LIFE WHEN YOU'RE WRITING?

I work full-time and have two small children, so rigorous scheduling is tough. Generally, I aim to write most days—even a few hundred words is progress. Late evenings and lunch breaks are my best chances to write. I also take notes and micro-write on my phone when I'm stuck in traffic or multi-tasking chores. I try to ensure I've gained some ground by the end of the week, though I don't stress myself out with specific word count goals.

WHERE DID YOU GET YOUR INFORMATION OR IDEA FOR YOUR BOOK?

My debut horror fantasy western novel, MELINDA WEST: MONSTER GUNSLINGER (Brigids Gate Press), came about after I wrote and published several short stories featuring a Bonnie-and-Clyde-like duo in the Old West. Because the story takes place during that historical period, I delved into archival papers and articles about the period to get a sense of interesting and appropriate details to include. This book falls into the "Weird Westerns" category— an Old West story with a speculative (science fiction, fantasy, horror) aspect.

APOLLO'S RAVEN

BY LINNEA TANNER

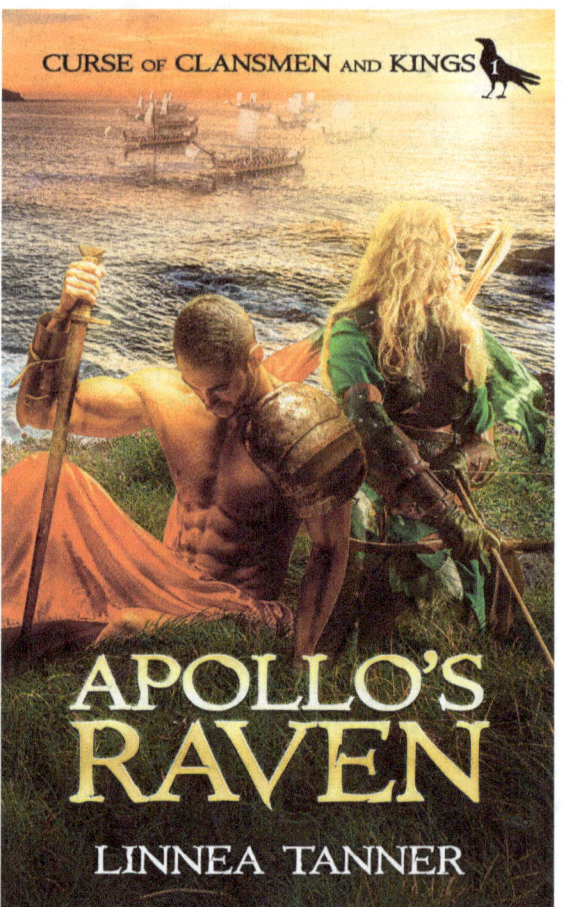

WHEN DID YOU FIRST REALIZE YOU WANTED TO BE A WRITER?

Since childhood, imaginary characters lived in my head and told me their stories. One was a female warrior reminiscent of an Amazonian from Greek mythology. Another character is her Roman lover, a military commander. I knew then that I wanted to be an author, but I still needed to pursue my dream. It was not until 2010, when I semi-retired, that I actively pursued my dream of becoming a published author.

HOW DO YOU SCHEDULE YOUR LIFE WHEN YOU'RE WRITING?

I'm fortunate to be semi-retired and not depend on a full-time job to make ends meet. Nonetheless, whenever I'm actively writing, I set a timeline to finish a book for publishing. I schedule quiet times to write and often work late into the night. However, I take breaks daily to do physical activities, such as walking and gardening, to clear my mind and do household chores.

WHAT WOULD YOU SAY IS YOUR INTERESTING WRITING QUIRK?

After taking a workshop on how creativity is enhanced by writing in longhand, I now draft all my scenes in longhand at the kitchen table. The scene projects like a movie as I write it in longhand. To set the mood for the scene, I often listen to movie soundtracks. After finishing the first draft, I type it into a manuscript template on the computer for further editing.

HOW DID YOU GET YOUR BOOK PUBLISHED?

I decided to independently publish my books under the business name Apollo Raven Publisher, LLC. Before publishing my first book, I researched the steps necessary to publish a quality book, then worked with a publishing expert to establish a detailed project plan to publish and launch the book. I contracted for other publishing services such as editing, interior formatting, cover design, and distribution at various retail sites.

THE GOOD LORD WILLING AND THE CREEK DON'T RISE: PENTIMENTO MEMORIES OF MOM AND ME

BY ROBERT W. NORRIS

WHEN DID YOU FIRST REALIZE YOU WANTED TO BE A WRITER?

In 1973, I hitchhiked across the States and bummed around Europe for a few months. I was a confused young man with no direction in life. Everywhere I went, I came into contact with young artists, poets, and musicians whose lives seemed filled with something important and meaningful. They all spoke more than one language. They motivated me to find some way to express myself. When I returned to the States, I began writing short stories and reading as much literature as possible. What started as therapy eventually became a way of life.

HOW DID YOU GET YOUR BOOK PUBLISHED?

After finally putting together what I thought was a polished manuscript, I began pitching it to different indie publishers. I must've sent it out to 50 places. A few expressed interest but eventually passed on it. Then Michael Cannings of Camphor Press answered my query and said that memoirs had been a tough sell for them, but if I were interested, he'd offer the services of a new hybrid press he was setting up. I'd considered self-publishing but decided to put the book in the hands of a true pro. I'm happy I did.

WHERE DID YOU GET YOUR INFORMATION OR IDEA FOR YOUR BOOK?

My entire life has been unusual and filled with the material to exploit. Most of my earlier fiction was at least partially autobiographical. My mother and I always had a strong bond and maintained lifelong correspondence. After she passed, I wanted to preserve her spirit and my memories of her. I had all these letters, e-mails, audio recordings of her family stories, videos, and all my earlier writing to use. It seemed natural to combine it into a story that captured both of our lives. The difficulty was in cutting out the excess.

The
GOOD
LORD
WILLING
and the
CREEK
DON'T
RISE

Pentimento
Memories of
Mom and Me

"An emotionally
powerful memoir
that spans nearly
a century and
several continents."

—Robert Whiting,
author of
You Gotta Have Wa

ROBERT W. NORRIS

BY STENETTA ANTHONY

WHEN DID YOU FIRST REALIZE YOU WANTED TO BE A WRITER?

I have always enjoyed recreating books I read but have yet to consider myself a writer. However, after being asked to develop a curriculum for my church's nursery department. The writer's bug hit because an original story had to be incorporated into this program. After this, my desire to write books began to grow and develop.

WHAT WOULD YOU SAY IS YOUR INTERESTING WRITING QUIRK?

Before my writing day, I listen to one of my favorite songs, dance for several minutes, relax, and start writing.

WHAT DO YOU LIKE TO DO WHEN YOU'RE NOT WRITING?

I consider several activities to be some of my guilty pleasures. I watched game and court television shows, spent time with my family, took long walks, and volunteered.

WHAT WAS ONE OF THE MOST SURPRISING THINGS YOU LEARNED IN CREATING YOUR BOOK?

When researching elephant traits, I learned. Elephants are the second longest-living mammal and have a life expectancy of 65 years, compared to humans, who are considered to live 73 years.

HOW DO YOU PROCESS AND DEAL WITH NEGATIVE BOOK REVIEWS?

Negative reviews can sometimes be disheartening. When I received my first negative book review, I was heartbroken. Yet, I have realized that every person will only enjoy my book with me. Thank the person for the review.

CAPTIVE

BY ROBERT P. FRENCH

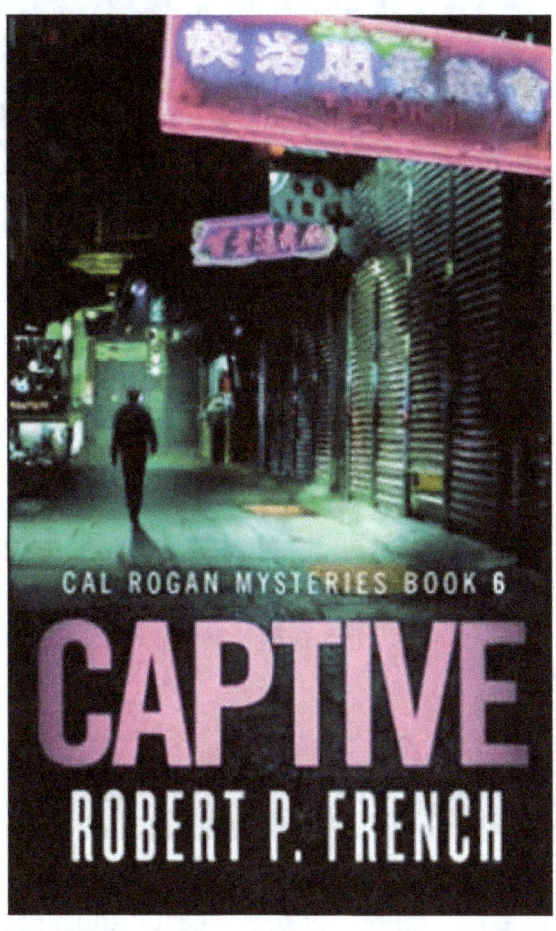

CAL ROGAN MYSTERIES BOOK 6

CAPTIVE

ROBERT P. FRENCH

WHEN DID YOU FIRST REALIZE YOU WANTED TO BE A WRITER?

In March 2003, the company into which I had poured my heart and soul was unable to get a new round of financing and had to close its doors. I spent the next day on the phone trying to find consulting work. At three o'clock, I opened a WORD document and started a book that had been in my head for a while. I wrote until the early hours of the morning. I was hooked. Although that book—and several subsequent attempts—never made it, I finally learned enough of the craft of writing to have a book worthy of publication.

HOW DO YOU SCHEDULE YOUR LIFE WHEN YOU'RE WRITING?

I dedicate two days a week to doing nothing but writing. In addition, I block off three hours a day, three days a week, as writing time.

WHAT WOULD YOU SAY IS YOUR INTERESTING WRITING QUIRK?

My dedication to little planning of a book. I prefer to let the story unfold as I write and not force myself to follow a set plan. Although this makes writing a novel more difficult (and frequently monumentally frustrating), the resultant unexpected twists and turns in the plot make it worthwhile. In my first book, Junkie, I did not decide who the murderer was until the book was 80% complete.

WHERE DID YOU GET YOUR INFORMATION OR IDEA FOR YOUR BOOK?

The idea came to me for Captive while I was reading a BBC News article on human trafficking. I did much research on the subject. In addition, I decided to set part of the plot in Hong Kong, and I had a wonderful time there getting to know the city.

GLOBAL BOOK

★ AWARD ★

An Interview with Author

Robert P French

Words of Wisdom

Me and my Writer's Block
CRAIG W. STANFILL

CRAIG W. STANFILL

TERMS OF SERVICE*

*SUBJECT TO CHANGE WITHOUT NOTICE.

Over the last couple of years, I have loathed and loved my writer's block. Sound familiar? If you're a writer, I bet it does. There is nothing so frustrating as sitting at the keyboard, day after day, unable to make progress. And yet, I have come to embrace it as an essential part of the process. Inevitably, if I have trouble writing a paragraph, scene, or chapter, the story I'm trying to tell is no good. I had initially set an ambitious goal for my second book, The Prophecy of the Heron, aiming to have it out less than a year after publishing it. At first, things were going great; I whipped through the nine Part I chapters in a couple of months. But then, when I hit Part II, I got bogged down.

I wasn't sure what the story was. I knew the end point — I'd already scripted out the climactic ending to Part II — but I didn't have a clear vision of how to get there. I banged out five more chapters, then got stuck for a good three months, unable to figure out how to make progress. The writing itself was fine; taken in isolation, each chapter was a good enough read, and yet the story seemed lifeless. And then, at last, I realized my mistake: one of the stronger supporting characters from the first book had been taken off the stage and could not liven up the action. I finagled the plot and brought my wildcard back early in Part II. It worked spectacularly well! I could make progress again, and although I would still get stuck on occasion, I was now in a better position to understand what I had done wrong and fix it sooner rather than later.

In the end, I'm glad I heeded my writer's block.

LIFELINE TO A SOUL

THE LIFE-CHANGING PERSPECTIVE I GAINED WHILE TEACHING ENTREPRENEURSHIP TO PRISONERS

JOHN K. McLAUGHLIN

The Book I Never Planned to Write
JOHN K. MCLAUGHLIN

I was taught early in life that if I wanted to accomplish something, the way to get it was to continue the pursuit until I achieved whatever I sought. This high level of determination has usually served me well. After building a successful business, I wanted to teach business courses. I was in my early 50s and had no teaching experience, and every job application I sent to a prospective employer was met with complete silence.

I spent seven years re-educating myself and applying to every teaching position I could find in a three-state radius until I finally landed the elusive first interview for an entrepreneurship instructor position at, of all places, a minimum-security prison camp. After walking through the prison yard and viewing the "classroom" where I would be teaching, I had severe reservations. I was so determined to teach, though I accepted the position and started a new chapter in my life. It was a great decision. I was given the freedom to construct the class the way I thought it should be and met some men with extraordinary potential who just needed a little direction and confidence to change the direction of their lives. My experience taught me that prisons, by design, dehumanize their denizens. It's the only way to run an orderly prison. However, this strategy does nothing to prepare the inmates ready to leave the prison experience behind them and work towards a brighter future.

Realizing we were in opposite philosophical camps, the prison staff significantly hindered my efforts the more I tried to instill confidence and hope in my students. When it finally ended, I told my father and his wife that I wouldn't have any more colorful prison stories for them. "You need to write a book about it," my Father's Wife's words hung in the air until I realized that was exactly what I would do.

We all have a story inside us worth telling and a receptive audience waiting.

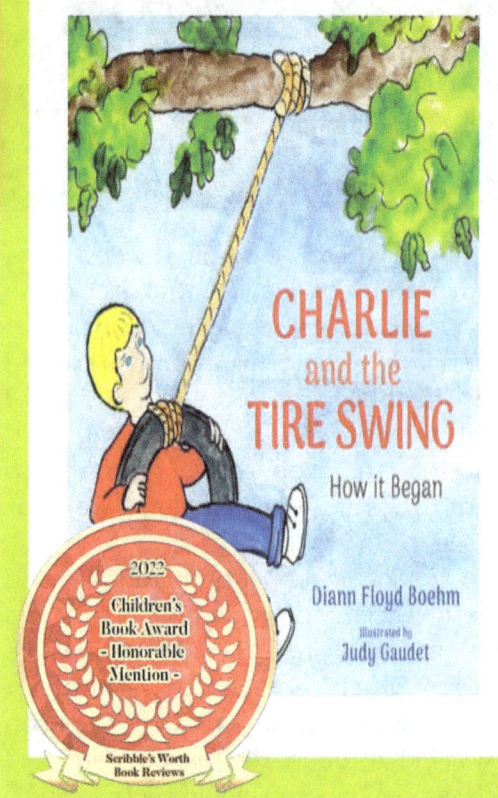

Me and my Writer's Block
DIANN FLOYD BOEHM

Imagination makes the world go round. I can't remember a day I have not enjoyed using my Imagination. My characters must be "Bold" no matter how great a role they play; I want them to be strong. My high school drama teacher, Mrs. Angelo, would stress to the cast that no matter how big or small your role is on stage, you have a purpose and must make your performance count. Even a "walk-through" in a scene is an essential part of the drama, or the playwright would not have included the character in the background. It is the same in writing a novel or children's book- to foster Imagination make your characters "Bold," and give them purpose! How can we create "Bold" characters with a purpose? Let's answer this in bite-size elements.

What is a "Bold" character in a story? A story's "Bold" character is complex and has many qualities, making nature multi-dimensional. Here are a few starting points.

One: Describe your character's appearance,

Two: What is their personality?

Three: Give your character a name; this will help make them real so readers can relate to them.

Four: Ask yourself - What is the "purpose" of the story? In other words, what do you want the reader to take away from the story?

Five: Write a back story for your characters. You do not need to include all or even some of the back story in your story, but knowing it is a valuable tool for you. A back story about my characters helps me understand why they make their decisions. You may model your characters after real people and design them around their personalities. Doing this helps drive the story and develop strong characters. The more authentic your feelings are, the more your reader will connect to your characters. You want your reader to want to know more and ask questions like, "What will happen next to this character? What are they feeling? How will they react?"

Enjoy bringing your characters to life, making them "Bold" and with a "purpose." And like I always say, "Embrace Imagination."

On Writing This Book
KI HYUN PARK

My first attempt to write anything worth mentioning started around when I went to live in Seoul, South Korea. It was my first time living abroad, and I recorded these experiences in journals and short stories, but nothing ever came to fruition, and I felt my writing was going nowhere. I decided to go backpacking to get over writer's block, and before the journey even started, I turned the trip into some writing with a definite beginning and end. Travel writing is helpful because the journey becomes the plot, and the report becomes reactionary, allowing you to record rather than invent. As my journey from China to Southeast Asia ended, I found myself with an exciting journal, but I wanted more than merely completing a travel diary. I went through a number of identity crises as a writer, wondering if I should aim to be serious or exploit a sense of humor, which comes naturally to me as a writer, especially in the pits of despair. After years of working on other stuff, I returned to the journey and decided to rethink and expand certain journal parts where I took creative liberties. For instance, the original book had a spy named "Jack Sour," who went through a sex change and even became a cyborg. Jack was a spin-off of a character named "Jack Bauer" from a show called "24", which I've never watched, but I liked the idea of a character being unhinged and screaming at everyone in a foreign country. He was meant to be the arch-rival of Sam Iam, but unfortunately, Jack never made it past the final cutting floor.

This anecdote might give a sense of where my book was ultimately headed, from a semi-serious treatise on travel and the misadventures of a guy bouncing around Asia without a map or itinerary to a book about sex-changing cyborg secret agents.

It's hard to say what the book was about in that middle evolution before its final form. Still, a lot was going on at the time: Trump was president, and the world was in a state of political division, unlike any other time I'd seen before. I began to sense that the book would find its place comfortably in satirical mode, and the travelers and the travel culture, which I had once wanted to laud as something extraordinary, now seemed indulgent and something to poke fun at, especially during the pandemic and the times of crisis we were headed in. Watching Trump be Trump gave further shape to the book as Candidate Dim started to take form, as well as members of Antifa, which formed the basis of the members of R.E.I.N.

It was an odd combination to place these American political elements into a story about traveling. Still, I was never meant to record anything that didn't sound like it could also be purely invented. Some things in the book happened, but I never did pull off anyone's toupee. I have a Beer Lao tank top somewhere that could double as a diaper. I've never actually tried that, but if I ever have a mushroom shake again in the wild, I certainly will.

Book Reviews

IMUE: FREEING MERLIN BY AYN CATES SULLIVAN

'Nimue' is a fantasy story about Nina venturing into a world filled with magical and mystical elements. The story revolves around Nina finding herself, who she is, and becoming the woman she is destined to be.

The literature is filled with much intrigue and devotion to the genre itself. While you are swept away into all the feelings and thoughts of the protagonist, you are also introduced to other characters that mesh very well with the storyline.

The dynamic of the tale is enjoyable to read. The mythology behind it and its feminine descriptive penmanship added a special touch.

The added romance was a bonus to the mix. I appreciated the protagonist being a woman. Her personality and demeanor were empowering for girls alike.

I recommend this book to fantasy and mythology readers.

Ayn Cates Sullivan, MA, MFA, Ph.D., is an award-winning and best-selling author. Dr. Sullivan is the president of Infinite Light Publishing. This small company focuses on books of mythology, folklore, and tales designed to make a positive difference to humanity and the living planet.

Ayn Cates Sullivan, MA, MFA, Ph.D., offers a unique blend of spiritual psychology, creative storytelling, color awareness, nutrition, and intuition as part of a soul-centered practice for the emerging time.

19

SWIMMING IN A SEA OF STARS BY JULIE WRIGHT

'Swimming in a Sea of Stars' is a fiction romance. The story begins with Addison and her emotional dilemma. She recently attempted suicide due to so much stress and insecurity. When she heads back to school, her fears of how everyone will react to her absence take over all she believes or is ready to handle.

The fictional tale introduces similar characters with different problems but all relatable and connected to the protagonist. The story has a nice flow, and the steady pace keeps the reader wanting to know what will happen next.

The book is mainly for young adult readers, and the dialogue, formality, and characters fully represent the genre.

I recommend this book to fiction readers and young adult fans.

Julie Wright (1972–still breathing) was born in Salt Lake City, Utah. She's lived in LA, Boston, and the middle of nowhere (don't ask). She wrote her first book when she was fifteen. Since then, she's written twenty-three novels and coauthored three. Julie is a two-time winner of the Whitney award for best romance with her books "Cross My Heart" and "Lies Jane Austen Told Me." The America Library Association listed "Glass Slippers, Ever After, and Me" in their 2020 top ten best romances and "A Captain for Caroline Gray" in their 2021 top ten best romances. Her book "Death Thieves" was a Whitney finalist.

Julie Wright has one husband, five kids, two grandbabies, one dog, and a varying amount of houseplants (depending on attrition).

She loves writing, reading, traveling, hiking, playing with her kids, and watching her husband make dinner.

She used to speak fluent Swedish but now speaks only well enough to cuss out her children in public.

FIREPROOF HAPPINESS: EXTINGUISHING ANXIETY & IGNITING HOPE BY DR. RANDY ROSS

'Fireproof Happiness' is a non-fiction self-help book written to derive happiness from hope. Dr. Randy takes you deep into the source of finding yourself and happiness regardless of how we make a situation, good or bad, influence us.

We all know what hope is and how it changes your perspective, but the author adds more to this feeling. It becomes a motivator and provides additional ammunition or assistance in pursuing happiness.

What stood out most in this book is how with the intention, it is written and the premise is organized. The literature is easy to read and understand. It has a nice flow to it, and you can follow through.

I appreciate the added personal touch. The author uses their experience and understanding of the subject, making it more relatable.

I recommend this book to those seeking happiness in life.

As the CEO of Remarkable and a former Chief People Officer, Dr. Randy Ross utilizes his experience to engage audiences worldwide with his keen insight and contagious humor.

Dr. Randy Ross is a compelling communicator, craftsman of culture, and bestselling author of multiple books, including Remarkable!, The Roadmap to Remarkable, Relationomics: Business Powered by Relationships and Fireproof Happiness.

Working with brands like GE Appliances, McDonald's, Cox Communications, Compass Group, Chick-fil-A, Panasonic, Keller Williams, and the Intercontinental Hotel Group, he has inspired and enabled countless people to find new passion and purpose in their work, work better together in teams and have more significant influence and impact.

THE MIDWIFE'S TOUCH BY SUE HARRISON

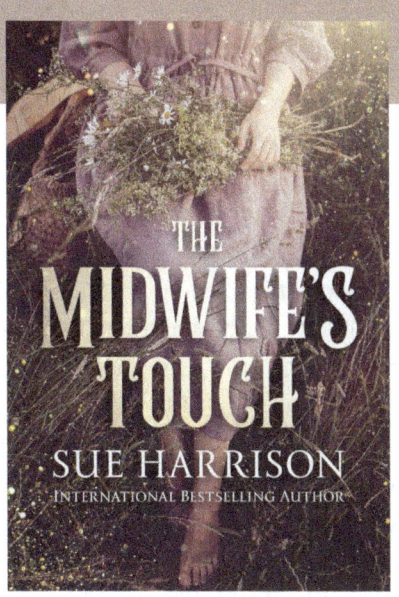

'The Midwife's Touch' is a historical romance about China Creed and her ability to grant wishes. Her power isn't just a blessing but also appears problematic; for this reason, her knowledge needs to be exposed to others. Things change for her after China's mom passes away. She is accused of witchcraft, and that is when the story picks up with an exciting chain of events.

What truly stands out in this book is the author's way of penmanship and storytelling. The content is filled with drama and depictions of prehistoric life as it has correct historical referencing. There is a particular talent embodied in her writing which is rarely seen, and this attracted me to read more.

I recommend this book to those who enjoy historical fiction and drama.

An international bestselling author, Sue Harrison has garnered recognition and critical acclaim for her six novels set in prehistorical Alaska, including the selection of her novel Mother Earth Father Sky as an American Library Association Best Book for Young Adults in 1991. Harrison's novels have been published in 13 languages and over 25 countries. Harrison lives in Michigan and Florida with her family.

Sue Harrison grew up in Michigan's Upper Peninsula and graduated summa cum laude from Lake Superior State University with a bachelor of arts degree in English language and literature.

FIRST SURVIVOR: THE IMPOSSIBLE CHILDHOOD CANCER BREAKTHROUGH BY MARK UNGER

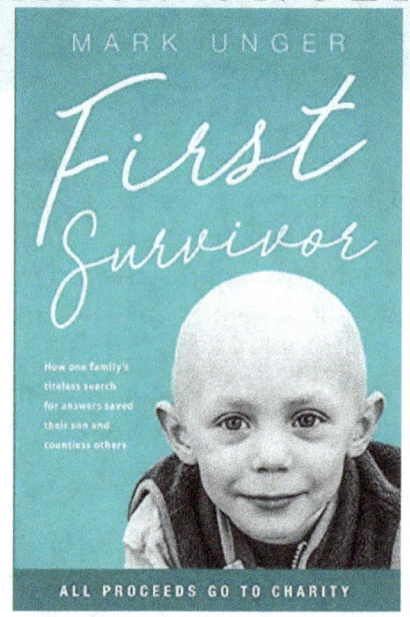

'First Survivor' is a heartbreaking story about Mark Unger and his son Louis' journey from being diagnosed with a condition with zero chances of survival.

The prominent point of this book isn't just for the parents to tell their story or for them to let you know that even with this overwhelming situation, there is always hope, but it is also because it introduces the Legg–Calvé–Perthes disease.

The added photographs and the beautiful conversations and thoughts between the family members were touching. The book invites you into their lives and all that they went through.

I found everything to be very well written and presented. I appreciated how the author shared everything in his book; others know they aren't alone.

I recommend this book to those who like to read biographies.

All proceeds from this book go to the Carrot Seed Foundation, where they will fund Neuroblastoma clinical trials and support the children and families stricken by this disease.

Mark Unger was born and raised in Solingen, Germany, where his mother and father owned a window cleaning tool manufacturing business. In 1978 the family moved to the United States, and Mark attended high school in Weston, CT, a picturesque town about an hour from New York City. After graduation, he attended Babson College in Wellesley, Massachusetts, and joined his family's business. In 1994 he married the love of his life, Mary Ellen Delaney. Their first son Harry was born in 1996, followed by Louis in 1998. Today, Mark and his family live in Bethany, Connecticut, where he is a Director and Owner of his family business, Unger Global, and is active in several charities. Mark and Mary Ellen enjoy traveling to explore new places, playing golf, fishing, and riding snowmobiles. And, of course, they love being with their sons, Harry and Louis.

THE SMARTEST PERSON IN THE ROOM BY CHRISTIAN ESPINOSA

In The Smartest Person in the Room, Christian Espinosa shows you how to leverage your company's smartest minds to your benefit and theirs. Learn from Christian's own journey from cybersecurity engineer to company CEO. He describes why a high IQ is a lost superpower when effective communication, true intelligence, and self-confidence are not embraced. With his seven-step methodology and stories from the field, Christian helps you develop your team's technical minds, so they become better humans and strong leaders who excel in every role. This book provides an enlightening perspective on turning your biggest unknown weakness into your strongest defense.

THE ROOT CAUSE AND NEW SOLUTION FOR CYBERSECURITY

THE SMARTEST PERSON IN THE ROOM

CHRISTIAN ESPINOSA

"This is an inspiring, enjoyable, fast-moving book that shows you how to unlock your full power for unlimited success." Brian Tracy, Author

THE UNFAKEABLE Code®

Take Back Control, Lead Authentically and Live Freely on Your Terms.

TONY JETON SELIMI
Multi-Award-Winning, #1 International Bestselling Author and Consultant

THE UNFAKEABLE CODE® BY TONY JETON SELIMI

Combining over 40 years of research, studies, and inspiring personal testimony, author Tony Jeton Selimi's enlightening advice will help you re-examine the rules, traditions, and thought processes that no longer serve you and provide you with a code to re-program your mind, take back control and live freely.

Designed to motivate, challenge, and inspire you to live on your own terms, this must-read book seeks to guide you on your path to self-realization and allow you to be more authentic at home, work, and beyond. If you want to let go of feeling powerless and out of control, it's time to discover the power of an Unfakeable personality.